HIDDEN L.A.

GIBBS·SMITH
P
PUBLISHER

Salt Lake City

Photographs by Alexander Vertikoff
Text by Robert Winter

HIDDEN

L.A.

First edition

01 00 99 98 4 3 2 1

Photographs copyright © 1998 by Alexander Vertikoff

Text copyright © 1998 by Robert Winter

Published by

Gibbs Smith, Publisher

P.O. Box 667

Layton, UT 84041

Orders: (1-800) 748-5439

Visit our Web site at www.gibbs-smith.com

The front cover art *Beaded Kitchen* is used courtesy
of the Peter and Eileen Norton Collection

Edited by Gail Yngve

Designed by Kurt Hauser

Printed in Hong Kong

Library of Congress Cataloging-in-Publication Data

Vertikoff, Alexander.
Hidden L.A. / photographs by Alexander Vertikoff; text by Robert
Winter.
    p.   cm.
ISBN 0-87905-741-6
1. Los Angeles (Calif.)—Pictorial works. 2. Los Angeles
(Calif.)—Description and travel. 3. Los Angeles (Calif.)—
Buildings, structures, etc. I. Winter, Robert, 1924- .
II. Title.
F869.L843V47 1998
979.4'94—dc21   98-18050
                    CIP

Page 1: Workman–Temple Homestead, City of Industry
Pages 2, 3: Tower of Pallets, Sherman Oaks
This page: Self–Realization Fellowship Shrine,
Pacific Palisades
Page 6: Keller Cabin, Solstice Canyon Park

Contents

Preface

Both of us love Los Angeles even though one of us now lives with his family in New Mexico and the other, an old bachelor, lives in Pasadena. This book arose out of our concern that most Angelenos take Los Angeles for granted, not realizing that we have a culture here. Part of it is off-limits to the general public and therefore hidden. A larger part is wide open to everybody, and yet it is passed by with little notice.

With all due modesty, we would like to do what we can to rectify that situation. We do so, we hope, without condescension. There is much in Los Angeles that we also overlook. One of us is a photographer who sees the place as full of objects that he pulls together by making a circle, pressing his right thumb against his index finger, and viewing objects in this frame. His camera spots pieces of the culture and gives us vignettes that tell many stories.

The other one of us, a historian, tries to see how these pictures fit together, but he is an architectural historian who, because of his limited perspective, misses a lot of the potpourri that Los Angeles contains. Nevertheless, the two of us hope that we together can open up a few vistas that have not been examined before. The central theme, we believe, is diversity, but it is not chaos. It makes sense. There is reason in our freedom.

The Penthouse–Oviatt Building

*t*he term *Art Deco* was derived from the title of a 1925 exhibition in Paris called *Exposition Internationale des Arts Decoratifs et Industriels Modernes*. It had been planned for 1915, but the Great War intervened, and it was put off until the twenties. The earlier intention is important because some of the designs date from that time. They suggest the

transition that was developing from the curving line of Art Nouveau to what David Gebhard has called the "Zig-Zag Moderne" for the ornament that almost always was the treatment at the roofline crest of buildings in this style.

The Art Deco style lasted only a few years, but it was terrifically popular in the age of the flapper and mooncalf. Thanks to the

westerner, it even invaded Shanghai, where several examples (the Archaeological Museum is one) ornament the skyline. Its appeal rests on its accessibility to the average person and is based on its relation to Gothic architecture, as in the tower of the old Bullochs Wilshire department store on the edge of the Central City, and at the same time its reference to the geometry that was seen as progressive and, thus, modern.

The penthouse on the thirteenth floor was presumably designed by the architectural firm of Walker and Eisen, who were the architects of the building's exterior. Other designers must have had a hand in the decoration of the 1928 suite, probably the New York firm of Feil and Paradise, which was responsible for the interiors of the men's clothing store on the first floor and also for some of the interiors of Bullochs Wilshire that were under construction at the same time. James Oviatt, the owner of the building and inhabitant of this ten-room apartment, had attended the Art Deco exhibition in Paris in 1925 and would have recognized Feil

and Paradise as leading advocates of this popular style.

The pictures of details from the living room, bedroom, and bathroom give only an incomplete idea of the richness of the decor. A description of the powder room (not shown here) was published in the *Los Angeles Times* on March 30, 1930: "A dressing room for feminine guests presents a symphony in the golden yellows of satin—-surfaced burl maplewood, fashioned into dressing tables and other conveniences with upholstery and hangings in gold and mauve." Every room was just as intensely decorated.

The penthouse is not easily seen unless somebody wishes to rent it out for a party, but the entrance to the building from Olive is in its own way just as spectacular as the thirteenth floor. The ceiling is covered with panels of Lalique glass. The elevator doors fashioned in an amalgam of copper, zinc, and nickel are faced with opalescent Lalique glass. The architects obviously knew what they were doing.

The Waterways

ater is the lifeblood of Los Angeles. It determined the site of the city, which was located near natural springs with the Los Angeles River not far away. Its emergence in the 1890s as a seaport came about because the city connected itself to San Pedro by a narrow corridor, incorporated the town within its own boundaries, and then built an artificial harbor in order to outdo nature. A milestone in riparian history was reached when in 1913 William Mulholland opened the cascade that let water from the Owens River into the San Fernando Valley. Later, other water suppliers were found that brought water to the Central City. It is not by chance that at the head of the present Beaux Arts Civic Center plan stands the Department of Water and Power Building, a sort of Parthenon symbolizing the city.

Water is also a problem. The dependence on aqueducts poses a threat from devastating earthquakes. The occasional years of heavy rains endanger the lowlands to the south, where even the concrete channels built to contain heavy runoff of the Los Angeles River do not ensure the area against flooding, and these concrete channels are so ugly that they are frequently the butt of criticism by people who would restore the whole ecosystem to nature.

In fact, the river and its tributaries, also with concrete channels, are so embarrassing to the public eye that they are largely erased from consciousness except when El Niño threatens. For example, the bridges across the Los Angeles River are usually ignored by most residents, even though they draw the city together. As a matter of fact some of them are beautiful from an aesthetic as well as an engineering standpoint.

Sepulveda Dam

The First Street Bridge is a fine neoclassical piece, complete with triumphal arches. A rather loose Gothicism applies to the Fourth Street Bridge. The Sixth Street Bridge is Art Deco. Those at Seventh Street and at Olympic Boulevard are less picturesque, but the Washington Boulevard Bridge boasts a frieze depicting bridge-building activities.

Even the fact that most of the year the concrete channels have almost no water in them has spurred creativity among the art-minded. The huge cat faces that have been painted around drain holes north and south of the Route 5 off-ramp at Glendale Boulevard are cases in point. An even more ambitious effort is the long mural that has been painted on the west side of the concrete channel of the Tujunga Wash, just north of the intersection of Burbank Boulevard and

13

Coldwater Canyon Avenue in North Hollywood. In 1972, the not-otherwise-inspired Army Corps of Engineers commissioned Judy Baca, a professor of art at the University of California, Irvine, to supervise the making of a mural that would depict the history of California. Baca sketched plans to be carried out by members of street gangs in a series of panels that were then touched up by trained artists. The murals were finished in 1983. So far there have been no floods to wipe them out.

Another obvious flood-control device is the dam. The greatest of these is the Sepulveda Dam, which can be seen from both the San Diego and Ventura freeways near their intersection but at such a fast clip that drivers are apt to miss this impressive sight. As in the case of other flood-control measures, this dam was designed and built in the 1930s by United States Army Engineers, and so the real designer is lost to anonymity. Whoever it was certainly understood what is called "PWA Moderne" in its streamline mode. The spillway has beautiful curved surfaces and the control tower even boasts round porthole windows.

The Sepulveda Dam is never used to produce power. Neither is it used in connection with water storage. As a result, the dam backs up to a large lowland area, some of it containing parks and golf courses but much of it simply uncultivated open space. In fact, this open space around the dam is about the only area in the San Fernando Valley that retains its once-rural character.

The Tower of Pallets

A few years ago, a member of the Cultural Heritage Board got a telephone call from a *Los Angeles Times* reporter: "Were you on the Los Angeles Cultural Heritage Board in 1978 when it declared the Tower of Pallets a Cultural Historic Monument?" the reporter asked. "If so, how in the world could the board have made such a strange decision?"

The board member said, "Well, there was precedent for it. We declared the Hollywood sign a monument. What other city would think of making a real-estate promotion a landmark? But, considering that Los Angeles has been a realtor's paradise, we thought our action was appropriate. The same kind of thinking applied to our decision in the Tower of Pallets case."

The reporter was not happy with that answer, so the board member tried to explain it. "You see, we thought that in a city of eccentrics, we should give credit to one of its greatest monuments to eccentricity."

The reporter didn't like that answer either. After a few more failed attempts to explain, the board member became angry and yelled, "Well, I guess we were all drunk!"

The reporter liked that response and printed it on the front page of the *Times*.

In 1951, Daniel Van Meter, the son of a scientist who had patented an oil-flotation process that made him rich, decided to build a tower over the grave of a little three-year-old girl who had died in 1869. The marker is still there. A friend had given him 2,000 pallets, the wooden platforms on which boxes of bottled beer are loaded before shipment, so Van Meter began piling these in concentric circles around the grave.

Eventually the tower rose to twenty-two feet.

Unfortunately Van Meter had not applied for a permit and, acting upon complaints from neighbors, two inspectors came from city hall. They declared that the tower was actually a fence and therefore needed no permit, though one of them did suggest that Van Meter get a giraffe to put behind the fence.

In the early days, the tower was visible from the street, but today it is all but hidden by trees and an assortment of things that Van Meter has acquired over the years. One has the feeling that this strange congeries will last only as long as its builder is around. He seems hale and hardy.

Blinn House

The Blinn House is truly out of place—the only house west of the Mississippi that was designed by George Washington Maher, a prominent Chicago architect and a friend of Frank Lloyd Wright, who shared an office with him when they were both young. Maher was particularly successful in getting commissions from rich Chicago businessmen, among them Edmund Blinn, a retired wholesale lumber dealer. Following the route of many midwesterners in search of a paradise, the

Blinns retired to Pasadena in 1905 and moved into their new house in 1906, having brought the expertise of their architect with them.

Maher got his early training in architecture in the Chicago office of August Bauer and Henry Hall and then worked for Joseph Lyman Silsbee. It was in Silsbee's office that he met Frank Lloyd Wright. Unlike many other young architects, he did not follow Wright into the Prairie style, although in several houses, he showed that he understood it. Most of his buildings are in

often carried his "organicism" into decorative motifs, such as using stylized sumac branches in the art glass throughout the Susan Lawrence Dana house (1902) in Springfield, Illinois, or in the actual plan of the Paul R. Hanna house (1936) in Stanford, California, where his hexagonal unit system is based on the structure of a honeycomb.

Maher never imitated any structures of nature, but he did adopt what he called a "motif rhythm" system of giving unity to a house by using a stylized natural form in the design of art glass and other detail. In the Blinn house he adopted a wisteria motif. The windows on the staircase landing and the mosaic on the living-room fireplace are cases in point. The latter was probably designed by the firm of Giannini and Hilgart, with whom he worked in Chicago.

As noted earlier, Maher was in love with the form of the segmental arch, a rather rare Roman device best seen in the colonnade around the Canopus at Hadrian's villa near Tivoli. It is almost his trademark, for he used it—perhaps too often—in almost all of his houses. It also gives a unity of feeling as noted in the door, the second-floor windows, and even the pergola.

the neoclassical tradition—heavily modified. They are usually symmetrical and explicitly show his fondness, as in the Blinn house, for the Roman segmental arch.

Strangely Maher saw his own work as progressive and, like Wright and Louis Sullivan, talked about a democratic architecture, an architecture for the people, but also like Sullivan and Wright he kept the meanings of *democratic* and *progressive* vague. He shared with Wright quite specific principles of design. For instance, Wright

The Koffee Pot
(formerly Hot-Cha Restaurant)

It is perhaps a commentary of our times that this piece of pop art, in spite of its signs to the contrary, is closed. It will probably molder away, for it is not in an area that the urban renewalists, who have made the western part of downtown Long Beach a disaster area of new but nondescript buildings, care very much about.

Although it is difficult to pin down sources of this kind of imagery, the design of this 1936 building seems to have been suggested by a drawing, patent number 83865, that is illustrated in Jim Heimann and Rip George's *California Crazy*. The drawing is attributed to Eugene L. Weaver of Los Angeles and is dated 1930.

Those interested should see the Koffee Pot as soon as possible, for it seems doomed.

The Workman-Temple Homestead

The appearance of these houses (and a cemetery) in the midst of buildings that look like computers made by computers is surprising. The homestead stands in a small but beautifully landscaped park so that by blanking out a few instances of the horrors of progress—faceless industrial blight and parking lots—one enters the world of yesteryear and, in fact, can easily imagine being in the country, especially with the distant mountain scenery as a backdrop.

Both the Workman and Temple families were early settlers on this land and were active participants in its development. At first they were ranchers, but in the aftermath of the Civil War they joined forces in the banking business, which encouraged the economic booms of the period. Together they were leaders in almost all phases of early Los Angeles life and in 1845 were further linked by the marriage of a Workman to a Temple.

William Workman, an English emigrant and the first of the Workmans in southern California, had in 1842 built an adobe on his property on the vast rancho once belonging to the San Gabriel Mission, and in the 1850s, after accumulating a fortune, began remodeling it. In the late sixties, he employed Ezra Kysor, one of the first architects to arrive in Los Angeles, to give him a house in the Italian-villa style that Workman had known in England and that was, at the time, becoming extremely popular in America. What Kysor gave him was a house with the round arches, quoins, and brackets associated with the building of country houses in England. Whether he realized it or not, Workman now had the accoutrements of an English country squire or perhaps a Spanish grandee!

The exterior of his home has been carefully restored, but the interior's only real refurbishment has been to hang the windows with lace curtains. The powers that be seem to be much more interested in the 1920s house next door, La Casa Nueva, as it is called. This was constructed by William Workman's grandson, Walter Temple, and his wife Laura. Aware of their connections with the Spanish past, the couple decided to build a house in the Spanish Colonial Revival style. They hired the prominent Los Angeles architectural firm of Walker and Eisen, but, becoming disenchanted with the architects' designs, they employed a young architect, Roy Seldon Price, who was lately from St. Louis but who had quickly understood the Los

Angelenos' craze for the Spanish image. He
had recently finished a house in Beverly Hills
for the movie director Thomas Ince, and he
now applied his experience with Iberian forms
there to the Temples' house. Especially
notable are the front door in a rather fluid
version of the Portuguese Manueline style
and the proliferation of Mexican tiles in
almost all the rooms of the house. The maker
of the art-glass windows that appear in many
parts of the house has not yet been
determined, but the restoration of some of
the windows that had been destroyed over the
years was carried out by John Wallis of
Pasadena, who certainly deserves credit. The
furnishings are mostly not original to the
house but are representative of the taste of
the twenties.

Nethercutt Collection

It all began in the 1950s when J. B. Nethercutt, chairman of the board and chief executive officer of Merle Norman Cosmetics, and his wife, Dorothy, bought a Model J Duesenberg and restored it not only to its pristine beauty but also to its original operating condition. After this first restoration, they acquired literally hundreds of old cars and eventually employed some twenty specialists to return them to working order and their original high style.

Naturally, the Nethercutts had to collect hundreds of hood ornaments, lamps, magnetos, and other paraphernalia in order to outfit the cars. To behold these in a magnificent showroom designed by Anthony Heinsbergen (even more are exhibited in a holding room on the ground floor) is to witness a re-creation of the history of the motorcar. Surely this is one of the finest automobile museums in the world.

On another floor is a different collection, this time of mechanical

musical instruments—organs, musical pocket watches, jewel boxes, player pianos, and a library of over 31,000 music rolls. The building also houses stained-glass windows—one designed by Louis Comfort Tiffany and another by Charlie Chaplin—and a collection of Louis XV furniture.

Under construction across the street is a 100,000-square-foot museum that will house a large portion of the automobile collection together with shops where visitors may see how the cars are restored.

All this is found in little Sylmar!

Gaudiesque House

SILVER LAKE

Very little is known about this Gaudiesque house, except that it is a remodeling of a house that was moved onto this spot; no one seems to know when. The present owner says that "a bunch of hippie types" were responsible for the application of the concrete and tile facade in the sixties. Obviously, the artist knew the work of Antonio Gaudí in Barcelona or at least was inspired by pictures of the Catalan's design for the Parque Guell. Another Gaudiesque structure was built in Beverly Hills, but it has been published often and lacks the louvered windows that give additional charm to this one.

The Old Mill of Banbury Cross

The Arts and Crafts movement was always teetering on the edge of the valley of the quaint. At the Old Mill of Banbury Cross, it makes the plunge. This house, completely invisible from the street, is one of the ornaments of the gardens that Adolphus Busch, the St. Louis beer tycoon, started to develop about 1904—the year after he bought the Cravens estate on Orange Grove Boulevard (then Avenue). The original gardens apparently consisted of about thirty acres to which Busch added parcels from time to time, so that eventually it stretched from Orange Grove Avenue on the east down into the Arroyo Seco on the west.

From the beginning, the gardens—mainly designed by Robert Gordon Fraser—were open to the public because, until his death in 1913, Busch had to curry favor with sober Pasadenans who did not like the idea of a brewer in their midst. After Busch's death, his widow, Lilly, kept the gardens open, but during World War I, her German name gave her as many problems as had the family's association with beer. Mrs. Busch, like her husband, tried to improve her image by featuring such patriotic affairs as a benefit for the Red Cross on June 15, 1918. From noon to midnight, a series of events took place. The Ruth St. Denis/Ted Shawn dancers performed. Madam Schumann-Heink—herself suspect since one of her sons was in the German army (another was in the American army!)—sang, accompanied by a chorus of 5,000 school children. The crowd dispersed at midnight after having sung "We've Come to the End of a Perfect Day" with the composer, Carrie Jacobs Bond, at the piano.

The Old Mill of Banbury Cross, now a private residence, apparently had no other function than being picturesque. One account says that it was built in 1890, well before Busch bought the Cravens estate. Whatever the date, it is clear the building was erected before his death since another contemporary newspaper story mentions his delight with it. At one time there was a sculpted stork on the roof, and the mill wheel used to be activated by a small stream. Around the mill and indeed throughout the gardens were fanciful sculptures of figures from fairy tales, such as Snow White, Cinderella, and Hansel and Gretel. Busch had sculptures like them at his home in Germany and remembered how children had loved them.

The Busch gardens remained a Pasadena institution until the late thirties when the Busch family sold the property to a developer who subdivided it. Some relics still remain in the yards that were once part of the gardens.

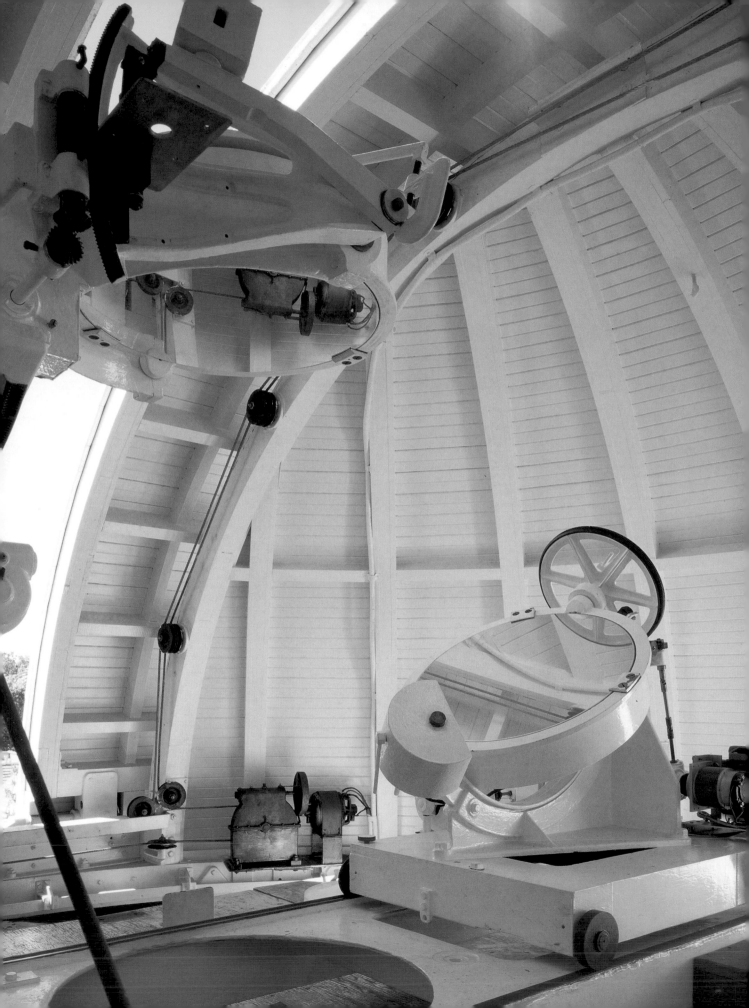

The Hale Observatory

In 1921, a little trade school in Pasadena called the Throop Polytechnic Institute became today's California Institute of Technology. Behind this metamorphosis one major figure stands out—George Ellery Hale (1868–1938), an eminent astronomer who had been appointed to the board of trustees of Throop and who, from the beginning of that relationship, had intended to transform it into the image of his own university, the Massachusetts Institute of Technology. It was he who suggested that Nobel Prize-winner Robert Millikan be its first president and who set Caltech on a course that would lead to its becoming one of America's greatest scientific institutions.

After graduating from MIT in 1890, Hale took a teaching job at the University of Chicago where he rose quickly to a professorship in astrophysics, a name he invented. The Carnegie Institution invited him to supervise the installation of a telescope on Mount Wilson near Pasadena and to be the observatory's director. He arrived in 1904 and almost immediately became a cultural leader, not only at Caltech but also in Pasadena's civic affairs.

Envisioning Pasadena as the "Athens of the West," he was chair of Pasadena's first planning commission and became active in developing its Beaux Arts Civic Center. With Chicago still on his mind, he also dreamed of an art museum that would resemble the Art Institute of Chicago. He even became a guarantor of the Coleman Chamber Music concerts.

On retirement from his work at Mount Wilson, Hale continued his research into the nature of the sun, particularly on its magnetic field and sunspots. With funds from the Carnegie Institution, he bought a piece of land from his friend Henry Huntington, and in 1924 built this personal observatory, furnishing it with first-rate equipment. The prominent Pasadena architectural firm of Johnson, Kaufmann, and Coate (Gordon Kaufmann was the architect of record) provided him with a building resembling an Arab-influenced Sicilian church. Over the massive front door, the firm placed an ancient Egyptian bas-relief of the sun, Hale's speciality. Inside the large library, there is a modern bas-relief by Lee Lawrie of Ikhnaton, invoking the power of the sun. Since he was interested in how various cultures interpreted the sun, Hale also exhibited a Mayan relief of the sun.

The gardens were originally laid out by the famous landscape architect Beatrix Farrand, whose husband was director of the Huntington Library. Most of the planting disappeared when the property was subdivided before the present owners took over.

Kimpson House

Long Beach is not noted for its early modernist architecture. Most of the city that has not been torn apart by urban renewal is devoted to bungalows of the teens and twenties, with the Arts and Crafts and Spanish Colonial Revival the main styles. A couple of large Beaux Arts hotels remain on the beachfront, and a little Art Deco still exists in the business section, but the city center has been botched by a medium high-rise that is a little worse than that of Brand Avenue in Glendale.

It is, therefore, a joy to find a distinguished example of the International Style in a neighborhood that is now largely 1950s mediocrity. The Kimpson house was designed by Raphael Soriano and built in 1939. Soriano worked in the office of R. M. Schindler, the Austrian expressionist turned Los Angeles modernist, for a short time and then longer for Richard Neutra, another Austrian emigre who brought the modern movement to Los Angeles. Soriano liked Neutra's clean lines and confessed himself incapable of understanding Schindler's strange forms. As Esther McCoy wrote in her *Second Generation*, "he [took] over Neutra's

framing, even painted the posts a steel color to match the sash. He also used Neutra's ribbon windows, his smooth stucco skin and flat roofs, his continuous fascia, the built-in furniture—always in-line, not Schindler's staggered volumes; he took over the low horizon line of the rooms, and the indirect lighting—even some of Neutra's awkward entrances, which required some side stepping when two guests and the host met at the front door."

When he designed the Kimpson house, Soriano had already been converted to the beauty of light steel-frame construction, but he would not have a chance to use it until after World War II. The house is wood frame and with a facade very similar to his 1938 Ross house in the Echo Park district of Los Angeles. It once had a view of a lake, but more recent building has left it without the natural setting. Incidentally, the beautiful Streamline Moderne house that stood next door to it and dated from about the same time has been mansionized into a nothing blob.

Paintings–The Flintridge Biltmore

In 1929, Myron Hunt designed this hotel high above Pasadena with a view of the San Gabriel Mountains and the Rose Bowl, of which he was also the architect. The hotel failed in the early stages of the Great Depression and was put to other uses.

In what was once the entrance hall, two paintings still hang, both commissioned by the builders and finished, like the hotel, in 1929. One depicts a band of Plains Indians who, it should be noted, never got that far west though the scenery in the background seems pure southern California. The other is even more curious—a procession of marchers, all wearing various national costumes, is advancing on the Los Angeles City Hall, which is imaginatively flanked by Bertram

Goodhue's Public Library, considerably elevated to seem to be another high-rise.

The details of both paintings deserve praise. Many of them—the yucca plants, the dappling on the coats of the horses, even the frames—are Art Deco. The artists, George Harold Fisher and Desmond V. Rushton, apparently worked together on both paintings, though who painted what is not apparent. Both were members of a circle of Los Angeles artists called "the Independents," an organization fostering, according to their stated aims, "Cubism, Dynamism, and Expressionism," though those qualities are not immediately recognizable in these rather static but wonderful images.

The Beaded Kitchen

FROM THE COLLECTION OF PETER AND EILEEN NORTON, SANTA MONICA

I am an artist, and I am going to bead the world," says San Diego artist Liza Lou about her idea of rendering common objects magical by applying thousands of tiny beads to their surfaces. She even contemplates attaching beads to the grass in her garden, a task that a mathematician friend believes will take approximately forty years.

The assemblage seen here in a private Santa Monica home takes its theme from a poem by Emily Dickinson that is affixed to the side of the stove.

She rose to his requirement, dropped
The playthings of her life
To take the honorable work
Of woman and of wife.

Kitchen, then, is a commentary on the plight of any woman in a labor-intensive occupation that is not recognized until it sparkles with beads—Lou's doing.

Something is owed to Ed Kienholz's sculpture; however, Kienholz invites one to come in and be a part of his work. Lou forces the viewer to stand off and walk around. Her application of beads seems to be an attempt to emulate the technique of Pasadena Rose Parade float makers—every surface is covered with flowers or parts of organic materials. Lou substitutes beads for petals.

An enigma, serious versus amusing, is intended.

The Flower Vendors Mural

When Millard Sheets joined the Scripps College faculty in 1932, he was an established painter in the Regionalist School of Los Angeles. His realistic watercolors and oils portrayed a jerry-built city that was also colorful in a brighter way than that delineated by the members of the eastern Ash-Can School that had preceded him and by which he was obviously influenced. He was greatly gifted but far from being in the avant-garde.

Sheets was at first the only member of the art department at Scripps, a women's college, then and now small by comparison to most colleges that have since made a go of it. What he proceeded to do in the thirties and forties was to assemble an art faculty that was remarkable when compared to almost any other academic institution in the country. At one time or another during this period, the painters Phil Dike, Jean Goodwin Ames, Henry Lee McFee, and Phil Paradise taught there. Sheets brought William Manker and later Richard Patterson to teach ceramics. Albert Stewart, a prominent sculptor from New York, was employed.

One of Sheets's many achievements was to bring the Mexican painter Alfredo Ramos Martinez (1872 – 1946) to the campus, not as a teacher but as an artist who would paint a mural on the wall of the Margaret Fowler Garden at Scripps. Martinez, trained in Mexico and Europe, had been important in fostering painting that emphasized Mexican subjects, thereby contributing to the cause of Mexican nationalism and preparing the way for such social-realist painters as Jose Clemente Orozco to develop their dramatic critiques of western civilization.

Martinez was not primarily a social critic although he was the Mexican minister of education during the revolutionary period and introduced plein-air painting in the Mexican school system. Artistically he was a simplifier in the realist tradition, as this mural indicates. Unfortunately it was never finished. Martinez died shortly after he had sketched it out and begun painting.

St. Anthony's Catholic Church

This church is a remodeling of the third St. Anthony's that was built here at the corner of Sixth and Olive. The first, a frame church constructed in 1904, was moved to 1851 Cerritos Avenue in 1923, where it still stands as Our Lady of Carmel, with beautiful stained-glass windows depicting the appearance of the Virgin at Guadalupe. The second church, which must have been built about 1924–25, was considerably more ambitious. Based upon pictures of it, there is a strong chance that the architect was Ross Montgomery, who also designed the Mausoleum of the Golden West in the New Calvary Cemetery and many other monumental Catholic buildings in the twenties. This second church was ruined in the Long Beach earthquake of 1933.

A new building, seismically secure, was designed by Emmet Martin—the brother of Albert C. Martin whose firm designed St. Vincent's Catholic Church at the corner of Adams and Figueroa in 1923—and Laurence Waller, another Catholic-owned firm. Then in 1954, the fiftieth anniversary of the parish's founding, the congregation decided to transform the structure. Employing the

architectural firm of M. L. Barker and G. Laurence Ott—of course, both devout Catholics—they sent to Rome for mosaics that would spice up the somewhat-tired facade and got the architects to build new towers.

The principal scene in the facade depicts the Virgin Mary's assumption into heaven. Watching this miraculous spectacle is Pope Pius XII and Los Angeles ecclesiastics Bishop John Cantwell and Cardinal Francis McIntyre.

The Roman mosaic, which took nine months to design and assemble, was then put together on the floor of St. Anthony's gymnasium by Monsignor Bernard J. Dolan (whose idea probably inspired it), a charming crew comprised of Fathers James Hansen and Leland Boyer, some sisters of the Immaculate Heart, and teachers from St. Anthony's High and Grade Schools. It took them three months to install it.

The work is astonishing, especially as it is flanked by Barker and Ott's towers, which are also covered with mosaics.

Japanese Gardens

Certainly the extraordinarily beautiful Japanese garden at the Donald C. Tillman Water Reclamation Plant in Van Nuys is a surprise since it is almost completely invisible from Woodley Avenue that runs past it. Inside the gate, visitors park their cars and enter the garden near the administration building of the facility, a handsome building (1984) by Anthony Lumsden in the toned-down New Brutalism that was characteristic of Los Angeles in the 1970s and early 1980s. Set against this formidable object, the subtleties of the garden, with its waterfalls, teahouse, bonsai pines, and assortment of waterbirds that are delightful under any circumstances, become even more expressive.

Another surprise is that on the other side of the Lumsden building are the sewage treatment vats. The architect has even provided a tower from which one can view the process at work.

Professor Koichi Kawana, who designed the garden in 1983, has written a pamphlet, given to visitors as they enter, that describes its organization in detail. He notes that his garden is "simple and abstract." It is beautifully maintained.

Across town in Bel Air is another Japanese garden, less authentic than the one in Van Nuys but just as beautiful. It was laid out by Nagao Sakurai over an older garden by A. E. Hansen dating from 1923. The transformation took place in 1961 and was given to UCLA in 1965.

Bigsby Tombstone—Hollywood Cemetery

In spite of twentieth-century attempts to socialize the cemetery, the contemplation of death still brings out the individualism of the deceased and his "loved ones." Carl Morgan Bigsby was intrigued by the Atlas Missile and asked that an exact marble replica in reduced scale be placed over his grave. His family complied with his request and erected a tombstone that includes vital statistics and a short estimation of the missile's significance:

First intercontinental ballistic missile

First to fly 8,500 miles November 28, 1958

First to lift a United States capsule into space

First satellite to broadcast a message to "the Free World"

First to record a message in space and rebroadcast it to earth

On the other side of the stone and directly over Bigsby's grave is the line "Retired by God" and nearby his wife's comment, "Too bad . . . but we had fun."

The Hollywood Cemetery, in whose center this missile exists, also contains the remains of other even greater figures. Because it's at the north end of the Paramount Pictures lot, it also attracted such greats as Cecil B. DeMille, Tyrone Power, Douglas Fairbanks, Jr., and even Rudolph Valentino, not to mention William Andrews Clark, Jr., whose neoclassical mausoleum was designed by Robert Farquhar, the designer of his library on West Adams (see essay on Clark Library). Harrison Grey Otis, the early publisher of the *Los Angeles Times*, is also there. Incidentally, the graves of all these stars and tycoons are marked with very tasteful monuments.

* FIRST INTERCONTINENTAL BALLISTIC MISSILE
  OF THE UNITED STATES

* FIRST TO FLY 5500 NAUTICAL MILES,
  NOVEMBER 28, 1958

* FIRST TO LIFT A UNITED STATES CAPSULE
  INTO SPACE

* FIRST SATELLITE TO BROADCAST A MESSAGE
  TO "THE FREE WORLD"

* FIRST TO RECORD A MESSAGE IN SPACE
  AND REBROADCAST IT TO EARTH.

BIGSBY

The William Andrews Clark Library

The Clark Library (1924–26) specializes in late-seventeenth- and early-eighteenth-century British books and manuscripts, so what could be more appropriate than to house them in a version of the late-seventeenth-century addition that Sir Christopher Wren made to Hampton Court Palace outside of London? The architect of the Clark, Robert Farquhar, was no plagiarist. He substituted yellow brick for Wren's lovely pink. Strangely, he omitted the decorative oranges that Wren had applied to honor his clients William and Mary of the House of Orange. Perhaps Farquhar thought that their inclusion in southern California would appear to be cheap commercialism, but the round windows on the second floor clearly owe a great deal to the similar treatment at Hampton Court.

Unfortunately, Farquhar's scaling down of Wren's building concentrates too much in a small facade and seems a little silly. Farquhar had a tendency to design well—the California Club in downtown Los Angeles is an

example—or poorly, but never in between. He was a graduate of the Ecole des Beaux-Arts in Paris, where he learned that the architect should work out the main functions of a building rationally and then cover them over with the kind of ornament that delights the eye. Here he seems to have let this rule get out of hand.

The interior is quite different. The marble entrance hall, with its glass cases exhibiting incunabula, tells visitors that they are in a library, as do the two rooms on either side of the hall. Nevertheless, most of the actual library is in the basement and in a subterranean vault running underneath the gardens originally designed by the distinguished landscape architect Ralph D. Cornell, who also planted the campus of Pomona College and that of UCLA, to whom the Clark Library now belongs.

The main attraction is the drawing room, which was originally furnished by George S. Hunt under the direction of Harrison Post. One cannot miss the fact that the ceiling, with paintings by Allyn Cox, who later worked on the Capitol at Washington, D.C., is voluptuously baroque while the walls are wood-paneled in flat English rococo. It is a beautiful room, rarely experienced even by users of the library.

The International Banana Club

ALTADENA

The banana is a crowd pleaser. Evidently the perfect food, it was bound to attract a zealot who would want to organize a club celebrating his favorite taste treat. The prime mover in this enterprise was Ken Bannister, or as he prefers, "Bananister." The International Banana Club, headquartered in downtown Altadena, is dedicated to promoting the message of the banana—keep one's spirits up and thereby maintain a positive attitude toward life.

Although there are no legal requirements for a lifetime membership, the fee is rather steep—twenty-five dollars—but one can join the bunch by acting quickly and sending ten dollars to the International Banana Club, Inc., 2524 North El Molino Avenue, Altadena,

California 91001. Membership entitles one to a club sticker, an iron-on "one of the bunch" transfer, and an issue of the *Woddis News* with its tips, bits, and tricks. Another benefit is being permitted to do graduate work toward an M.B. (Master of Bananistry) or a Ph.B. (Doctor of Bananistry) degree, the level depending upon the number of banana-related items the member sends to the Top Banana. As he says, "Everyone likes special titles and degrees."

Featured among the 17,000 banana-related items inside the museum are such gadgets as a golf putter in the shape of a banana, the "Michael Jackson banana" covered with sequins, and a picture of an athlete doing a banana split.

The museum is located at the above address near Lake and Mendocino and is open by appointment only. It can be reached either by telephone (626) 798-2272 or by e-mail—BananasTB@aol.com. The web site is http://www.BANANA-CLUB.com.

Church of the Angels—Garvanza

Its exterior is completely open to the street but, picturesque as that is, the real treat is the interior of this church, usually open only for Sunday services and weddings. Everything inside the church is almost dollhouse in scale and just about everything is old. Except for floors and lighting, little has been changed since 1889 when the church was built.

It was commissioned as a memorial to Alexander Robert Campbell-Johnston by his widow, Frances. Campbell-Johnston, a rich Scot, had bought the Rancho San Rafael and settled his sons and their families on it. Upon his death, Mrs. Campbell-Johnston went back to Britain and selected Arthur Edmund Street, the son of George Edmund Street,

one of the greatest English Victorian architects, to design a version of his father's Holmbury St. Mary's Church near Dorking in Surrey.

Frances Campbell-Johnston brought the plans back to southern California and entrusted them to another Englishman, Ernest A. Coxhead, to adapt them to the site. Coxhead virtually changed the entire design so that the church is really his. The beautiful stained-glass window that depicts the open tomb of Christ after his resurrection was fabricated by Cox, Buckley, and Company of London. Appropriate biblical references are incorporated in a frieze at the top of the walls. The diminutive scale is accented by a tiny baptistry at the rear of the church. Near it is a lovely memorial mosaic (1889) in pure pre-Raphaelite style. As in all fine architecture, the details are everything.

Not long after designing the church, Coxhead moved to northern California, where he became one of the major Arts and Crafts architects of the Bay Area shingled houses. He also became the unofficial architect of the Episcopal Church in California, designing wonderful (and slightly mad) churches from Red Bluff to Santa Ana.

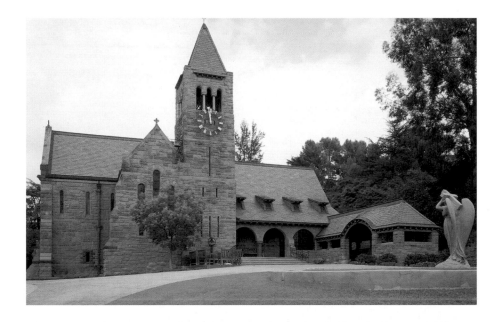

Aztec Hotel

Anybody who knows anything about history realizes that the decoration on this hotel is Mayan, not Aztec. According to his own account, the architect Robert Stacy-Judd knew the difference, but, having business savvy, he believed that the general public was more familiar with the Aztec civilization than with the Mayan. He thought the name would attract guests as they drove by on the old Route 66 that passed right in front of it.

Stacy-Judd was an Englishman trained in the office of an architect in Sussex. After serving an apprenticeship, he struck off on his own, designing a number of awkward-looking houses and public buildings, among them three theaters in the Egyptian Revival mode. This experience evidently interested him in large aggressive-looking forms.

According to his autobiography, Stacy-Judd had always wanted to move to North America. In 1911, he sailed for Quebec, but after a short time in Canada, he moved to Minot, North Dakota, where he designed a number of rather tired-looking buildings. After World War I, he moved briefly to Canada, but he found little work there and returned to the United States, where he set up a practice in Hollywood. There, the prospects seemed brighter. Indeed, soon he was engaged to design several west-coast hotels by the Hockenbury Systems, Incorporated, of Harrisburg, Pennsylvania. About the same time, he bought John L. Stephens's two-volume *Incidents of Travel in Central America, Chiapas, and Yucatan* (1841), with its wonderful woodcuts designed by Frederick Catherwood to illustrate Mayan ruins.

When Stacy-Judd showed the book to his clients in the hotel business, they agreed with him that decoration of the hotel in Mayan fantasies would certainly attract tourists' eyes. He claimed that he was the first to exploit Mayan decoration in modern architecture. Such statements are inevitably foolish. Frank Lloyd Wright had employed Mayan motifs as far back as 1915 in his German Warehouse at Richland Springs, Wisconsin, and before him they had been used by Paul Cret in the well-published Pan American Union building (1908–10) in Washington, D.C.

Whatever Stacy-Judd's claims, there is no question that the Aztec Hotel is a significant testimonial to the widespread search in the 1920s for a modern "American" architecture that was indigenous to the Western Hemisphere. This search was widespread in the ventures into period revivals.

The hotel was internationally famous in its time. Now, although well-maintained, it is largely ignored by people who travel along Foothill Boulevard, which is no longer Route 66.

Tower Room, Los Angeles City Hall

The Los Angeles City Hall (1926–28) was designed by three major architectural firms—John C. Austin, John and Donald Parkinson, and Albert C. Martin. It is difficult to see how any agreement could have been reached by the squadron of architects that must have been involved except for the fact that the building is, on its exterior, very bland and impersonal architecture. The austerity is somewhat relieved by the stepped pyramid of the roof, which is based on a conjectural reconstruction of the tomb of Mausoleus at Halicarnassus. More importantly, the prototype seems to have been agreed upon—the Nebraska State Capitol by Bertram Goodhue—built just a few years earlier.

The interiors are also bland except for the rotunda on the third floor, the council chambers, and the mayor's office, which were designed by the young architect Austin Whittlesey. They are all open and fairly familiar to Los Angelenos, but the Tower Room on the twenty-seventh and top floor is not. Although not as gorgeous as his other work, the interior of this room, marvelous for cocktail parties, is also probably by Whittlesey.

Another tie with Goodhue is that just under the cornice on all four sides of the room are edifying inscriptions by the University of Nebraska philosopher Harley Burr Alexander, who developed the ideological program for Goodhue's Nebraska Capitol and also for his Los Angeles Public Library. Their spirit is well encapsulated in one of them: "The city came into being to preserve life; it exists for the good life."

As of this writing, the Tower Room is closed for repairs of damage caused by the Northridge earthquake, but those interested can be assured that the money is in hand to restore it and reopen it to the public. Its space is very grand, and the views from it are magnificent on a smog-free day.

High Ornament

LOS ANGELES

It has always seemed surprising that, in the Beaux Arts high-rises of the turn of the century and later, so much expense was put into decorating the top floors. The ornamentation is not usually seen by pedestrians, but only by people who have views from about the same height. When architecture was lower and horizontal, there was some purpose in giving a kind of finishing off in the gables or cornices, but the retention of such ornament can only be understood as a tradition that was preserved in the tall buildings of the early twentieth century and then significantly dispensed with

in the later modern movement, which argued that "ornament is crime."

Much of the ornamentation can be enjoyed particularly in Los Angeles, where so many Beaux Arts works exist on Spring Street, Broadway Avenue, Hill and Olive Streets, and Grand Avenue. Incidentally, such elevated bric-a-brac is relatively rare in San Francisco, which has lost a great deal of it since its downtown district was rebuilt in the modernist manner. Outside of Los Angeles, only in New York can so much attention to the tops of early tall buildings be found.

These buildings are just a few examples from the Central City. Many more building tops can be seen there simply by lifting one's eyes toward the heavens.

Bridges Hall of Music,
or Little Bridges

Pomona is the oldest and most prestigious of the six institutions that comprise the Associated Colleges group. It was founded in the village of Pomona in 1887 by Congregationalists who were confident that the land boom of that year would be sustained and their college supported. In fact, the boom immediately collapsed. The fledgling college had to find quarters and finally settled into a new hotel in nearby Claremont that had closed for lack of patronage. It was thought that the tenancy would be temporary, but even with the return of prosperity in the 1890s, Pomona College stayed in Claremont.

At first, a few new buildings were added near the original Sumner Hall (the old hotel). Then in 1910, the architect Myron Hunt was employed to give some coherence to the campus. He used the plan of Thomas Jefferson's University of Virginia as a prototype, collecting the proposed buildings around a central green and incidentally moving Sumner Hall to a new position to the south.

The plan was not adhered to over time, but the finest of Hunt's designs for it, Little Bridges (1915), was erected. His work, early and late, was somewhat dry and without ornamental detail, but here he chose a triumphal arch as the central motif for the facade and flanked it with protruding buttresses topped with dramatic volutes. In the interior, the classrooms are quite simple in ornament, but their Spartan detail is contrasted with an ornate auditorium full of decorative juice.

The building is significant as premonitory, even before Bertram Goodhue's San Diego Fair of 1915, of the Spanish Colonial Revival that was to drive southern California architecture in the 1920s. Facing onto a small street to the north and set behind other buildings, its magnificent facade is almost never seen by visitors to the campus.

Fine Arts Building

Reflecting the growth of population and the economic boom after World War I, the period of the twenties was a great age for the building of public and commercial structures in Los Angeles. It follows that the demand for architects grew. In fact, while in 1920 about 124 architects practiced in the city, by 1929 their number had increased to 270. As their numbers grew, so did competition for commissions, assuring clients that their architects would carefully supervise the construction work on their buildings. Add to this the demand of clients that the construction costs must be low while the buildings must be eye-catching, and one has a partial accounting for the high standards of the architecture of this period. In addition, one also understands why Los Angeles, even today, is considered a twenties city.

The Fine Arts Building (1925) is a monument to the prosperity of the age. The firm of Walker and Eisen that designed it was one of the large architectural offices in the city. Employing fifty draftsmen when their closest competitor, Parkinson and Parkinson, had an office of only eighteen, it built such major structures as the Beverly-Wilshire Hotel (1926), the James Oviatt Building (1927–28), the Title Insurance and Trust Building (1928), the Texaco/United Artists Building (1927), the Mar Monte Hotel (1927) in Santa Barbara, as well as the Fine Arts Building, to name only the most salient of their works that still exist.

The Fine Arts Building faces Seventh Street assertively with its facade almost a stretching-out of the Romanesque front of the cathedral at Lucca. Like most twenties fronts of commercial buildings in Los Angeles, the detail is terra-cotta, crafted by the Gladding-McBean Company in Lincoln, California. Walker and Eisen had intended to use stone, but that being excessively expensive, the architects decided to "out-stone stone with a texture material having diversity of color . . . and giving crispness of ornament." Albert Walker himself is supposed to have said that "the aim was to achieve an architectural mass that would afford a broken skyline without those deep setbacks that mean a loss in rentable area."

The exterior of the Fine Arts Building is there today as crisply as it was in the twenties for everybody to see and enjoy, and so is the lobby, though few people besides the tenants go inside. Visitors will find a cathedral of decorative tiles designed by Ernest Batchelder of Pasadena, certainly one of his largest commissions. All the ceramics—from the sculptural figures on the balcony level to the hands on the floor indicators above the elevator doors—were designed by him and cast in his kilns.

El Molino Viejo

SAN MARINO

Tucked away behind a wall in a fine residential district so that many of the people of San Marino don't know it's there is one of the oldest buildings in Los Angeles County. The Old Mill (1816), as it is called in English, was one of the outermost dependencies on the far-flung San Gabriel Mission lands. It was a flour mill powered by a horizontal waterwheel that was activated by a stream flowing through the property. Inefficient, it was abandoned in 1823 when a new mill was built immediately in front of the mission's main buildings. None of the machinery remains except for two millstones that can be seen in the gardens.

Its original use gone, the building served as a recreation center where picnics were

often held. In 1859 it was given by its owner, Thomas White, to his daughter Fannie and her husband E. J. C. Kewen, who used it as their home. The Kewens built a Greek Revival porch on the east side and made other improvements, as did its subsequent owners.

Rumors of buried treasure on the property caused the building to be vandalized many times until 1903, when Henry Huntington bought it and installed a caretaker. Then in 1914, it was turned into a clubhouse by Huntington's architect, Myron Hunt, who restored it imaginatively, removing additions and replacing the shingled roof with tiles from an old adobe in Santa Barbara.

It was used as a clubhouse for the Huntington Hotel golf course until in 1927 it was acquired by Huntington's former daughter-in-law Mrs. James Brehm, who called in building contractor Frederick H. Ruppel to make the house livable. This entailed considerable alterations, providing a dining room where the mill wheels had been and a staircase to the upper floor. Other changes were made, such as installing a fireplace near the main entrance. Painted decoration was added near the baseboard in the upper room. Wide-plank flooring in the style of the twenties was also laid. It's uncertain what else has been done.

It may seem that this building has been renovated so many times that it would have lost the patina of age. In fact, a good deal of patina has been added, including stripping off the stucco in some areas of the exterior walls to show the construction of volcanic rock, fired bricks, and adobe. Nevertheless, it remains one of the really fascinating buildings in Los Angeles, never mind that the Spanish would never have thought of it as architecture!

First Church of Christ, Scientist

Charles Moore (1925–93), the architect of this church, was one of North America's finest designers in the sixties, seventies, and eighties. His first widely published building was the Condominium I (1965) at Sea Ranch, a housing development on the ocean about a hundred miles north of San Francisco. In it and later buildings at Sea Ranch, he used simple barnlike forms that fit beautifully into the lush landscape.

In the seventies, he moved from simplicity into a kind of baroque madness often associated with the postmodern movement. Probably the most bizarre manifestation of this tendency was his Piazza d'Italia (1975–78) in New Orleans, where, using his knowledge of Italian architecture—from Hadrian's Villa at Tivoli to Mussolini's cruder rendering of classicism—he fashioned an assemblage of forms, including neon signs, that defied all canons of taste.

In the eighties, he continued his play with history (he had a Ph.D. in architectural history) but a seriousness crept into his work. The first sign of this mood came out in the art gallery he designed for Dartmouth College in the early eighties. Here a committee of about thirty people, drawn from the student body, the faculty, and the town of Hanover, helped him design a building that connected a Richardsonian Romanesque structure with one of Wallie Harrison's adventures into "barrel vaults and modern shapes," as Moore himself phrased it. His aim, as he said, was to become a good neighbor to both buildings. Incredibly, he did.

Left: St. Matthew's Episcopal Church (1982–83) in Pacific Palisades was Charles Moore's first attempt to work with an entire congregation acting as a building committee.

The First Church of Christ, Scientist in Glendale is a product of this more conservative bent. As at Dartmouth, he took his clients, this time the entire congregation, into consideration. Two Christian Science churches had decided to sell their old buildings and use the money to build a new church suited to their unification. Why they chose Moore as their architect is not known except that the denomination is known for its occasional rejection of the Beaux Arts neoclassicism of the mother church in Boston for adventures into less conventional imagery, for example, Bernard Maybeck's Christian Science Church at Berkeley.

The Glendale church is a product of Charles Moore's maturity. It is as if he had studied Mary Baker Eddy's *Science and*

Health and rendered something that he thought she would approve. She surely would do so if she were to see it today.

Moore was a funny man. There is no major axis in this church—nothing really on which the photographer can focus, nothing to draw everything together. Those who knew the architect now realize that he was in total control of the situation. He got the effect he wanted. According to the custodian who was on hand when the church was being planned, Moore stood in the center of the site of the future auditorium to frame the heads of the existing palm trees in his windows. The design is distracting and, at the same time, one of the most serene works of his career.

The Camposanto—San Fernando Mission

SAN FERNANDO

The San Fernando Mission was founded in 1797 by Fray Fermin Francisco de Lasuen, the seventeenth mission in the chain that extended from San Diego to San Francisco. Few of the buildings in the rather elaborate assemblage are old, the *convento* completed in 1822 being the oldest. Most of the rest were reconstructions of the original buildings imaginatively restored by Mark Harrington in the 1920s. The church was horribly damaged in the Sylmar earthquake in 1971 and rebuilt on the Harrington model with a magnificent Spanish altarpiece being added.

The grounds and buildings, with their furnishings and books from the old days, are a major tourist attraction, but few pilgrims go through the door in the north side of the church. It leads to the *camposanto* where 2,449 Native Americans were buried from 1797 to 1846. Recently a simple cross has been erected, eloquent testimony to early California history.

Petal House

One example of International Style architecture can be found in this book—the Kimpson House by Raphael Soriano. It is all chaste and pure—in fact, too much so for a number of architects whose works begin to appear in the seventies and come into their own in the eighties. Unfortunately, their work has been called "postmodern." It does not take a logician to explain that nothing can come after modernism because modernism always refers to the present.

However, a little joke is being played here. One assertion of International Style practitioners was that, being based entirely on geometry and functionalism, the style was without style, and the implication was that the procession of styles had come to an end— no more Tudor or Spanish Colonial Revival. In fact, a number of pedants recognized the problem inherent in the phrase "International Style" and adopted another term, *modernist*, which was intended to cover the same ground but to avoid the style issue. Of course, this nominalist movement has caused just as many problems as before, including the absurdity of the term *postmodern*, which simply means an antagonism toward the dogma of the International Style.

Consequently, Eric Owen Moss, the architect of the Petal House (1982), is called a postmodernist, though he would deny it. He knows the International Style and builds on its geometry, but he also goes beyond it in being playful with its formality.

Here, in this remodeling of a simple tract house, he adds a second story, using siding and shingles like that in the original house and those around it, but then he fools around with the roof. Imagining that it might be pyramidal, he peels back four triangles and sets them at differing angles so that they appear to be like petals on a flower. It certainly isn't International Style.

The Mausoleum of the Golden West

NEW CALVARY CEMETERY, EAST LOS ANGELES

The New Calvary Cemetery is more than a place to inter corpses. It is a piece of social history. Old Calvary was near the civic center of Los Angeles. Its closing in the 1920s mirrored a need for commercial space, but its removal to what was then the city limits also reflected a concern, originating in the early nineteenth century, for the health of the city dwellers. Germ theory was not developed until the 1870s, but before that the Victorians realized that what they called "bad air" or "the vapors" had something to do with sickness, and so they stopped burying in churchyards and created new cemeteries on the fringes of urban development where they would presumably cause no harm.

By the twentieth century, this idea had been developed into the notion of a cemetery as a rural park, an association of the earthly paradise with the heavenly paradise, a return to Eden. In turn it offered the living a chance to escape the city. The cemetery with its green grass, flowers, and trees was considered a haven from the heartless world. It remains so today, even for people who attack the absurdity of Forest Lawn. In fact, the criticism of that Los Angeles institution usually results from the cemetery representing a form of materialism that dishonors the dead.

Until the memorial park concept advanced to the notion of open spaces with green lawns, cemeteries were vast arrays of grave markers and elaborate tombs that signaled the wealth and taste of the deceased and their loved ones. They were monuments to individualism and the cult of personality. The new idea, at the nineteenth century's end, of placing simple grave markers flush with the ground not only improved the view (and incidentally removed the monument as an impediment to lawn mowers) but also subordinated individual to social needs. As the undertakers' journal *Modern Cemetery* put it bluntly in 1890: "Civilization consists in subordinating the will of the individual to the comfort and well-being of all." Cemetery superintendents, it argued, had the expertise to identify the social will and carry it out.

Nevertheless, the urge to create elaborate monuments continued. In a sense, the mausoleum was the solution to the problem. With its vault-lined halls, the vaults set on either side like filing cabinets, it accommodated many corpses, freeing the rest of the cemetery to become a garden. On the other hand, its grand size offered the possibility of architecture on a large scale and with generous figurative allusions.

The Mausoleum of the Golden West is a case in point. Designed by Ross Montgomery, the semiofficial architect of the Catholic Church in the 1920s, the central dome is based fittingly on one of the reconstructions of the tomb of Mausoleus at Halicarnassus. The wings of the building house small crypts, the doors to which resemble Roman or even Etruscan designs, and the row of angels supported on Roman columns are obviously the heralds of the Second Coming.

Once inside, visitors will note that the chapel at the top of a staircase resembling one out of a motion-picture palace is a little disappointing, but the vaults contain the remains not only of bishops but also such people as Irene Dunne and John and Lionel Barrymore. Ethel is there, too, but in a nearby hallway.

Struckus House

Certainly this is one of the most unusual buildings in Los Angeles County if not the world. It was one of the last works that Bruce Goff (1904–82) designed, and it shows him at peak form in merging the liberal imagination of his clients with his own creative madness.

Goff showed early talent in drawing, so much so that at the age of twelve, he was apprenticed by his father to the Tulsa architectural firm of Rush, Endacott & Rush. There he learned to be a draftsman—the nitty-gritty of architecture—and also was given the opportunity to trace Palladio's Basilica at Vicenza, along with the completely different lines of Frank Lloyd Wright's Unity Temple at Oak Park. That was his training.

Probably the greatest influence on Goff's point of view was Frank Lloyd Wright—not Wright's style or details but his wide-ranging eclecticism in searching for forms that expressed the patterns of his own soul. Wright drew on historical sources at will or experimented with materials in order to express his freedom. Goff also experimented with materials. Nevertheless, however bizarre his concoctions, he understood construction.

His buildings were buildable, though he surely had gifted friends in the construction business. His eclecticism came from the unexpected: turkey feathers, gold lamé, and even poultry inseminators were the devices he used in order to assert his principles. Sometimes the results seem postmodern, but they really are not a part of any historical movement.

In the foreword to David G. DeLong's fine biography of Goff (1988), Frank Gehry, summarizing Goff's life and work, wrote "He enjoyed opportunities to explore his vision, to extend it, to experiment and contribute architecturally through a fine, comprehensive practice and career." The Struckus house (1979) illustrates the fact that even in old age Goff was still expanding his imagination. Why it should look like a tree with blisters or, as David Gebhard noted, an eighteenth-century birdcage, is not the point. Goff was just beginning to roll.

Il Giardino della Vita

In 1982, Norman Neuerburg gave up his teaching responsibilities at California State University, Dominguez Hills, and, like Candide, literally retired into his garden on a terraced hill in his backyard. A well-traveled man, he had seen many very personal gardens in Europe and decided to emulate, not the actual elements found in them, but the spirit and whimsy of his predecessors. He has said that Hadrian was his model— but Hadrian on a small scale if that can be imagined.

Actually his garden is a series of vignettes held together by the fantasy of its designer. He collected mostly small things that he found in various parts of the world and put them together in a way that gives them a meaning known only to himself. Of course, this tone of mystery allowed him to regale the astonished onlooker with a series of stories that relate to experiences in his life; thus, the title he gave to his assemblage translated "Garden of Life"—his life, his garden.

He wrote:

Occasionally paint, some pieces of lumber or a few bricks had to be purchased, but only as final touches to complete objects and shrines largely built of existing materials, of pieces left over from past projects or salvaged and scrounged over the years. Also included were ceramics acquired on trips going back to my days as a soldier in Italy at the end of World War II, pieces I made in Italy in 1949 and 1964 . . . even cattle bones collected on an adventurous visit to Baja, California—Pismo clam shells, glazed terra-cotta ornaments from a demolished bank, a marvelous antique jar given to me by my uncle, and even a memento of my father—a sign with a pigeon, publicizing his vocation/avocation as a breeder of fancy pigeons. In a way [my garden] is a collection of notes for an autobiography.

Neuerburg continued to work on his garden of life almost to the day of his death: "Every morning when I get up, I first go to the window and look out and see what I have been able to do, and I think, Life is good."

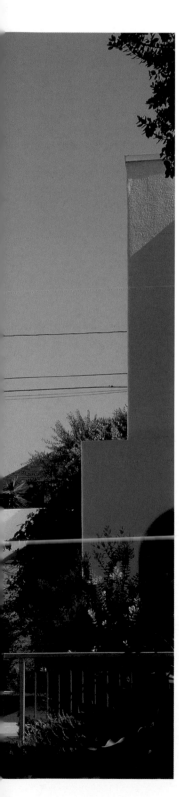

Irving J. Gill (1870–1936), the architect of this apartment complex (1919–21), had worked for a short time for Louis Sullivan in Chicago. He moved to San Diego in 1892, and, seeing Mission Revival architecture going up all around him, he remembered Sullivan's admonition that in order to reform architecture it might be best to do away with ornament and get back to the essentials—construction and geometry. Amusingly, Sullivan was never able to practice what he mildly preached, but apparently Gill saw this insight as a way of liberating the Mission Revival from its awkwardness while retaining its reference to the indigenous past.

Significantly, Gill did not always relieve the mode of its awkwardness, designing proportions both on interiors and exteriors that are often strange. Yet the process of elimination, resulting in geometrical volumes, made many of Gill's buildings seem curiously close to the contemporary modernist architecture developing in Germany in the early twentieth century, though there is no concrete evidence that Gill was influenced by Walter Gropius or any other purveyor of the new aesthetic.

If there was a source other than the Mission Revival, it was the adobe architecture of the Southwest that Gill knew. The Mission Revival had always been suspect as superficial and awkward, but the multiunit structures such as we can see today, principally at Taos, New Mexico, were admired by early twentieth-century travelers, as were Navajo rugs and Acoma ceramic bowls.

The general arrangement of the buildings of the Horatio West Court are reminiscent of Pueblo architecture, but notice that Gill retains the round arch of the Mission Revival.

L os Angeles has always been a religious center. The fact that so many of its first families moved there for the miracle of good health would serve as a basis for spiritual development. The universal appeal of a beneficial climate would also attract a diversity of background and belief. Even the get-rich-quick spirit would foster an individualism that could be diverted into introspection.

This lovely park, now the property of a religious organization, is a tranquil place to work out problems without being interrupted by proselytizers or people soliciting money.

Chances are that most residents of the Los Angeles area have passed it many times and thought they might stop someday. Then they got caught up in the traffic where Sunset meets the Ocean Highway and never took the opportunity to investigate its beauties.

In the 1920s, the land was an outdoor setting for Inceville movies. It was sold in 1927 to Alphonzo Bell, Sr., a real-estate developer, who brought in machinery to grade the hills so that houses could be put in. Apparently this scheme was a victim of the Great Depression. A large basin had been dug, which soon filled with water from

abundant springs, but no real development occurred until Everett McElroy, a construction executive for Twentieth-Century Fox, bought the land in 1940 and began to transform it into his dream:

. . . looking up at the bowl surrounding my mudhole, I could see terraces of trees— all kinds of trees, maybe 500 tropical and otherwise. I could see banks of flowers and shrubs and a path meandering around the lake, with cutaways into the bank for tree ferns and hanging baskets of fuchsias and begonias and mossy green rock plants. I was itching to build rockeries and put in rustic wood bridges and a giant water wheel that would act in conjunction with a pump as irrigation through a pipe-laid water system over the whole project.

The McElroys brought in their house-boat, *Adeline*, from Lake Mead and then built their own picturesque house across the lake from where the boat was moored. A Dutch windmill completed the architectural work until a new owner sold the property to the Self-Realization Fellowship, an ecumenical religious order devoted to the recognition of the "common faith in the Fatherhood of God," as it was expressed by its leader, Paramahansa Yogananda, who brought together symbols of all major religions. He even acquired a portion of Mohandas Gandhi's ashes and set them in a shrine on the grounds.

Adamson House

Technically speaking, the Adamson House (1928–29) was designed by the firm of Morgan, Walls, and Clements, but by the time it was built, Morgan and Walls had retired, and Stiles Clements became the architect of record. It is a rare example of the firm's domestic work that was known largely for its commercial buildings, such as the Richfield Building (1928), the Samson Tyre and Rubber Company (1929), now known as the Citadel, and the Wiltern Theater (1930–31), all of which Clements designed.

The house is a fine, if not exceptional, example of Spanish Colonial Revival architecture and is situated on one of the most beautiful Pacific beaches to be found in southern California. But the really exciting part of the place is the use of quantities of decorative tile from the Malibu Potteries, which had its factory on the beach not very far from the house.

Rhoda Adamson, whose husband Merritt had founded the Adohr (Rhoda spelled backwards) Farms Dairy Company, was the daughter of Frederick Hasting Rindge, one of the great land developers in southern California. When her father died in 1903, he left his vast estate to his wife, May, who, in order to keep it together, launched several enterprises, among them the Malibu Potteries.

May Rindge looked around for an expert in ceramics to manage her company and found Rufus Keeler, who had opened his own firm in South Gate—the California Clay Products Company (Calco). His experience coupled with Rindge's money gave him the opportunity to use his imagination in developing some of the most original and colorful 1920s tile designs produced in southern California.

It was natural that the Adamsons would use products from the Rindge's tile works in building their house. Most surprising are the special installations found throughout the building. Probably the best example of these fascinating displays is a facsimile of a Persian rug that is rendered in tiles and placed in the hallway between the dining and living rooms.

The Huntington Tomb

SAN MARINO

Thousands of tourists flock to the Huntington Library and Gardens every year. It is the only place in Los Angeles that has descriptive circulars in Spanish, Korean, Japanese, and English, but few visitors ever see this tomb (1927–29), the prototype—on a smaller scale—for the Jefferson Memorial in Washington, D.C., located on a bank of the Potomac.

A number of years ago, S. N. Behrman wrote a still-delightful biography of Joseph Duveen (Lord Duveen of Millbank), an art dealer to American millionaires. In it, he tells a hilarious story about how Duveen "educated" Henry Huntington into an obsession for purchasing Gainsborough's *Blue Boy* and other eighteenth-century paintings magnificently displayed in the Huntington Gallery today. Huntington was grateful and often consulted Duveen on other artistic matters.

When in 1927 Huntington was thinking of a monument to himself and his late wife, Arabella, he asked Duveen for advice on who might design it. Duveen recommended the American architect John Russell Pope, with whom he was working on plans for the great gallery that now houses the Elgin Marbles at the British Museum in London. Pope, a former fellow of the American Academy at Rome and graduate of the Ecole des Beaux-Arts in Paris, got the job. Huntington wrote joyfully: "The model arrived in perfect order. It is, indeed, a great work of art, and I have never seen anything in modern architecture that appeals to me more than this does. It is a great classic and just the type I dreamed of." Huntington died before the tomb was finished, but his staff saw that the plot was planted with specimens of his favorite tree — the lemon eucalyptus — and that John Russell Pope's name was inscribed on one of the steps of the tomb.

Anyone who has ever traveled by railroad in Europe, Asia, or even in America realizes that a train ride is one of life's most romantic diversions. Perhaps that experience is behind our excitement over model railroads. They bring back memories of interchanges with strangers, small towns viewed after dark through the Pullman window, the long wail of the warning horn, people sorting themselves out according to tracks in the train shed. There is still a touch of excitement in an airplane ride, but it is nothing like the thrill of the layers of adventure provided by the train.

This model railroad club has about 50 members that operate what they call the Sierra Pacific Line. It goes from a fictional midwestern city called Alhambra through such intermediate cities as Colton, Delta, and Echo and ends up in the port city of Zion (A to Z). It takes about fifty minutes to traverse this route unless you catch the bullet train that travels twenty times the speed of a normal train and completes its journey in about eleven minutes.

The large area that is devoted to this apotheosis of transportation also includes a narrow-gauge logging train and a trolley line along with such related facilities as a steel mill, marshaling yards, and a seaport. More is to come.

Los Angeles has always depended on its water resources, but the railroad made possible the great city that it is today. This model railroad has a symbolic meaning as well as being a lot of fun.

Acknowledgments

We thank the people who helped us in so
many ways to do our work, including Fran
Anderson, Ken Bannister, Bill Barmore, Sally
Barngrove, Diane Boysen, George Brumder,
Norman Cohen, Jacqueline Coulette, Mary
Ann Eldridge, Margaret Eley, Sam Frias,
Edward Garlock, Father Robert Gaestel,
Judith Goodstein, Loxie Hagthrop, Trish
Keefer, Susan Lee, Ruthann Lehrer, Don
Lewis, Troy Lewis, Liza Lou, Peter and
Eileen Norton, Skip Marketti, Jay Oren,
Robert L. O'Rourke, Pat Orr, Merry Ovnick,
Mary Beth Pope, Mary A. Roberts, Barbara
Ryan, Ingeborg Sept, Christine Shirley,
Barbara Thornburg, Sally Thornton,
Max Van Balgoy, Daniel E. Van Meter,
Micheline Vogt, Monsignor Francis Weber,
and Romy Wyllie.

Thanks also go to our editor, Gail
Yngve, who has disciplined us without ever
pressing us too hard, to Kurt Hauser and
his wife Grace, who have done the graphics
and given us a beautiful book, and to Jean
Viggiano, who has been our patient and
loyal typist.

In addition, we would like to thank
the institutions that opened their doors to
us, including Appleton and Associates;
William Andrews Clark Library; First
Church of Christ, Scientist, Glendale;
Pasadena Women's City Club;
St. Matthew's Episcopal Church, Pacific
Palisades; The Nethercutt Collection; and
The Peter and Eileen Norton Collection.